THE GREATEST SHOE ON EARTH

Other SHOE books by Jeff MacNelly:

The Very First SHOE Book
The Other SHOE Book
The New SHOE
On with the SHOE
A SHOE for all Seasons
The SHOE Must Go On

by Jeff MACNELLY

An Owl Book

HOLT, RINEHART AND WINSTON   New York

Library of Congress Catalog Card Number: 85-81673
ISBN: 0-03-005613-6

First Edition

Printed in the United States of America
1 3 5 7 9 10 8 6 4 2

ISBN 0-03-005613-6

A REPORTER IS ONLY AS GOOD AS HIS SOURCES AND HIS FILES...

— SO IT'S GOOD TO HAVE A SYSTEM YOU CAN BE COMFORTABLE WITH.

HERE, KID...PUT THIS IN THE JUKE BOX...

PLAY ME B·19... IT REMINDS ME OF MY GIRL...

DARLIN', TRACE THIS CALL.... I DON'T KNOW WHERE I AM..

DO YOU REALIZE WE HAVE A 200 BILLION DOLLAR DEFICIT IN THIS YEAR'S BUDGET?...

WOW.

HOW MUCH IS THAT IN PIZZA?

WE NEED A REAL GRABBER FOR A FRONT PAGE PHOTO...

WELL, THERE'S THIS SHOT OF SENATOR HELMS PUNCHING OUT THE SOVIET AMBASSADOR...

OR THIS ONE OF THE CHINESE PREMIER AT DISNEYLAND— THAT'S HIM WITH THE MOUSE EARS...

A GREAT ONE OF AYATOLLAH KHOMEINI THROWING OUT THE FIRST GRENADE AT THE INTERNATIONAL FESTIVAL OF TERRORISM...

PRINCE OF WALES AND LADY DI HUNTING SNIPE IN SCOTLAND WITH FLAME THROWERS...

AND THIS SHOT OF PRESIDENT REAGAN WITH A STRAWBERRY CONE STUCK TO HIS FOREHEAD...

IS THAT IT?...

YEAH... EXCEPT FOR THIS ONE: SOME BIMBO IN A BIKINI— PLAYING FRISBEE WITH HER LABRADOR...

JUST DON'T CROP THE LEGS.

TAKE ONE AND PASS THEM BACK!!

GOOD GRIEF!! THE HISTORY FINAL!!

HERE'S WHERE I VIOLATE THE BAN ON SCHOOL PRAYER.

GIVE ME STRENGTH, O, LORD!!...

AND A BIG SHOVEL FOR THE ESSAY QUESTION.

AS LONG AS THERE ARE HISTORY EXAMS...

WE'LL ALWAYS HAVE PRAYER IN SCHOOL.

I WANT TO GIVE YOU AN UPDATE ON YOUR EMPLOYEE BENEFITS.

YOU'LL NOTICE THE PENSION FUND IS UP 72% OVER LAST YEAR.

THIS IS DUE TO THE EFFORTS OF YOURS TRULY,

DIRECTOR OF YOUR PENSION FUND,...

—WHO MADE SOME REMARKABLY PRUDENT INVESTMENTS.

WE DID OKAY IN COMMON STOCKS, PUT SOME IN BONDS,...

AND PICKED UP A REAL BUNDLE...

WHEN WE HIT THE TRIFECTA AT BELMONT RACEWAY.

SHOE

WE'RE STANDING AT THE CROSSROADS, MY FRIENDS!!...

THE FREIGHT TRAIN OF PROSPERITY IS ROLLIN' DOWN THE SILVER RAILS...

ME FIRST

AND WHEN IT PULLS INTO THAT JUNCTION WE CAN EITHER CLIMB ON BOARD, OR WE CAN WATCH IT RAMBLE ON DOWN THE LINE!!

IT DON'T MATTER IF YOU'VE BOUGHT A FIRST CLASS TICKET...

OR IF YOU'RE THE PORTER OR THE FIREMAN, A CONDUCTOR OR EVEN THE ENGINEER...

OR EVEN IF YOU'RE A HOBO HUDDLING IN THE CORNER OF THAT DUSTY, EMPTY BOXCAR SWAYING IN THE NIGHT...

ME FIRST

THAT SPEECH WILL NEVER GET HIM TO THE WHITE HOUSE

E SYS OVERN PEOPL

BUT IF HE CAN SET IT TO MUSIC HE'LL MAKE IT BIG IN NASHVILLE...

AGAIN AND AGAIN I REITE THE LENGTH AND BREADTH THIS MAGNIFICENT LAND C

MacNELLY

BOSS! I GOT THESE FANTASTIC PHOTOS OF THIS BLOODY COUPE IN NORTH CAROLINA!!...

WHAT?! YOU MEAN THERE WAS A COUP IN OUR OWN BACKYARD?

THAT'S RIGHT!! AND I GOT THE PICTURES RIGHT HERE!!

EIGHT SHOTS OF THE COUPE ITSELF!

YOU MEAN COUP... IT'S PRONOUNCED "COO"—GOOD GRIEF! THIS IS A MASSIVE NEWS STORY!!

GET ME OUR FOREIGN CORRESPONDENT IN RALEIGH!!

NO, I MEAN COUPE...

A BLOODY COUPE.... LIKE I SAID.

SEE, THIS FARMER RAMMED HIS '54 CHEVY INTO THIS ELM HERE... WORSTEST NOSE BLEED I EVER SAW...

MacKELLY

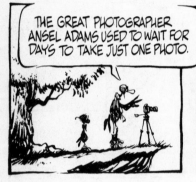

Boston Destroys New York, 14-2.

Milwaukee Bashes A's, 10-1; 12-0.

Baltimore Decapitates White Sox, 11-1.

Mets Murder Giants, 17-2.

Cubs Demolish St. Louis, 14-2.

Padres Rip Guts Out of LA, 15-0.

Rangers Eaten Alive By Indians, 13-0.

?

Pirates Quite Rude to Atlanta, 4-1.

WHAT THE HECK, IT'S JUST A GAME.

TODAY'S BRIEFING DEALS WITH OUR BOLD EFFORTS TO DEVELOP DEFENSIVE SATELLITES IN SPACE.

—THE SO-CALLED "STAR WARS" SYSTEM.

NOW, YOU SKEPTICS SAY THAT IT CAN'T BE DONE—WE CAN'T DEFEND THIS COUNTRY WITH THIS COMPLEX NETWORK OF BUCK ROGERS STUFF THAT HASN'T BEEN INVENTED YET...

WELL, YOU SAID THAT ABOUT PUTTING A MAN ON THE MOON...

YOU SAID IT ABOUT THE SHUTTLE...

WE ACCOMPLISHED THOSE MISSIONS, GENTLEMEN, AND I'LL SHOW YOU WE CAN AND WILL ACCOMPLISH THIS MISSION, TOO...

BY UTILIZING OUR HIGH-TECH CAPABILITIES AND GOOD OL' AMERICAN KNOW-HOW!!

COULD WE HAVE THE FIRST SLIDE, LIEUTENANT!

◎☆#?!!

BOOOF

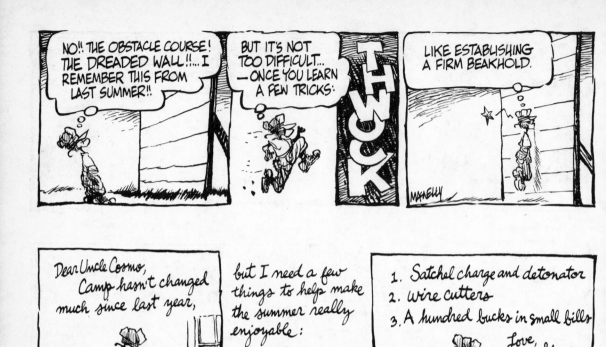

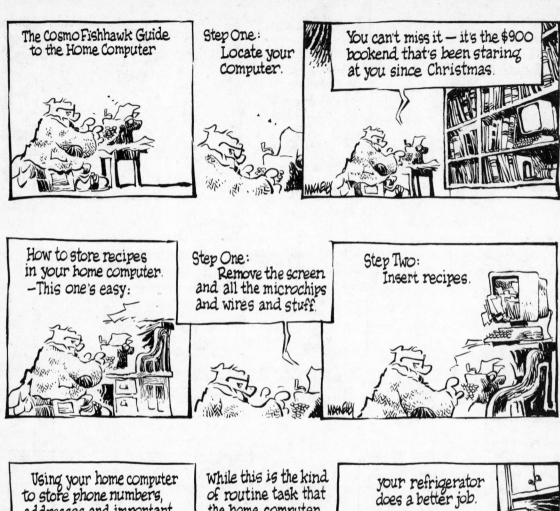

Using the computer to help productivity on the farm:

Step One:
Reprogram chips and wires and floppy disks by interfacing with any trashmashing system.

Step Two:
Insert moist soil and fertilizer...

Remember, your home computer can be your good friend.

By tailoring it to the needs of your individual lifestyle,

you can have a high-tech source of constant pleasure and relaxation.

The home computer can also be helpful with your hobbies...

Capt. Clevis P. Transom of Barnstable, Mass., uses his computer to help him build his ship models.

YEP! NO MORE THREADING THEM TINY PARTS THROUGH THE NECK OF A BOTTLE...

More uses for your old home computer: The aviation industry has relied on computers for many years...

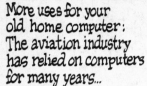

but recently, airlines have discovered that small home computers are very useful, too...

as high tech wheel chocks.

PERFESSER? WOULD YOU...

LOOK, I'M ON DEADLINE...CAN'T IT WAIT??

EEEP EEP

SURE... SORRY.

50,000 GRINGONS!! EXCELLENT SHOOTING, STAR COMMANDER!!

EEP...

Your Home Computer in the Library.

Dictionaries are very bulky and hard to handle when you're looking up a word. But now ...thanks to the computer revolution,

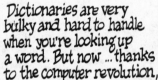

we have the word processor to rest it on.

Dear Uncle Cosmo
    Some kids go to camp to hike and swim....

or they go to basketball camp to play basketball...

or tennis camp to play tennis

or computer camp to learn all about computers...

Some kids go to Drama camp to act and dance and sing.

Some even go to Fat camp to get skinny...

but I go to Boot camp...

and get kicked around.

WHY DO WE HAVE TO GET UP AT O DARK HUNDRED JUST TO SHOOT DUMB BIRDS?

THESE AREN'T YOUR NORMAL BIRDS.

YOU HAVE TO GET OUT REAL EARLY TO TRACK DOWN THE BIRDS IN THIS COUNTY.

NOW STAY LOW... THIS IS THE SPOT.

THEY SHOULD BE COMING OUT SOON.

DO YOU REALIZE IT'S ONLY 4AM?

I KNOW.

BUT WHAT KIND OF TIME IS THAT TO BE STALKING BIRDS?

CLOSING TIME.

G'NIGHT, GUYS!...

BAR

THE RELIEF ACE IS ON THE MOUND—TWO ON, TWO OUT... BOTTOM OF THE NINTH...

LOOKS TO HIS CATCHER FOR THE SIGN...

FIST—FAST BALL... NO THANKS... THE KID SHAKES IT OFF...

TWO FINGERS— THE SLIDER—WRONG PITCH IN THIS SITUATION...

THREE FINGERS?!... NOPE, I CAN'T SNAP OFF THE CURVE THIS LATE IN THE GAME... I'LL HAVE TO SHAKE THAT OFF, TOO...

WHAT'S THIS?...

TIME OUT!!

I BETTER GET THESE SIGNALS STRAIGHT...

WHAT THE HECK IS THE THUMB FOR?

IT'S FOR STICKING IN YOUR EYE IF YOU DON'T HURRY IT UP AND THROW SO WE CAN GO HOME!!

HAVE YOU EVER NOTICED HOW BALLPARKS ARE A LOT LIKE THEIR CITIES?...

FENWAY PARK IS OLD, SORTA LOPSIDED AND RAUCOUS — JUST LIKE BOSTON.

THEN THERE'S YANKEE STADIUM.

IT'S HUGE, AWESOME AND EXPENSIVE — JUST LIKE THE BIG APPLE.

AND LOOK AT WRIGLEY FIELD... IT'S SOLID, WORKMANLIKE, WITH A NEIGHBORHOOD FLAVOR THAT JUST SAYS "CHICAGO."

YOU CAN FIND OUT A LOT ABOUT A CITY BY GOING TO THE LOCAL BALLPARK.

LIKE THE TREEDOME HERE. WE PLAY A UNIQUE BRAND OF BASEBALL IN COLORFUL SURROUNDINGS...

WHICH TELLS A LOT ABOUT US AS A COMMUNITY...

RIGHT.

ESPECIALLY WHEN WE USE THE WINO FOR THIRD BASE.

SHOE

WHAT'S GOIN' ON AROUND HERE?

WE'RE PRACTICING FOR THE MEDIA OLYMPICS.

WE DECIDED THAT WE FOLKS IN THE MEDIA SHOULD HOLD OUR OWN OLYMPICS...

SO WE'RE FIELDING A TEAM FROM PRINT MEDIA TO GO AGAINST A TEAM FROM TV.

WAIT A MINUTE... HOW ARE YOU PAYING FOR ALL THIS?

NO SWEAT. WE'RE HARNESSING THE POWER OF OUR FANTASTIC FREE ENTERPRISE SYSTEM,

WITH A BOLD DREAM AND A CRAZY FAITH IN OUR SUCCESS.

—AND IN THE TRUE SPIRIT OF ENTREPRENEURSHIP THAT MADE AMERICA WHAT IT IS TODAY, WE'LL RAISE MONEY THE OLD-FASHIONED WAY:

WE APPLIED FOR A GOVERNMENT GRANT.

MacNelly

WHAT'S THAT?

A SUBPOENA. THE JUDGE WANTS TO SEE MY NOTES ON THAT CORRUPTION STORY I DID...

ARE YOU GONNA LET HIM HAVE 'EM?

I CAN'T...

YOU KNOW THIS COULD MEAN THE SLAMMER FOR YOU, BIG GUY?...

YES.

GOOD FOR YOU!! WE'LL TAKE THIS THING ALL THE WAY TO THE SUPREME COURT IF WE HAVE TO!!!...

AMERICA NEEDS MORE CITIZENS LIKE YOU—WITH THE GUTS TO STAND UP FOR FREEDOM OF THE PRESS AND THE FIRST AMENDMENT!!

WELL, I'M PROUD OF YOU. GOSH, REFUSING TO GIVE UP YOUR CONFIDENTIAL NOTES LIKE THAT—IN THE FACE OF A CERTAIN JAIL SENTENCE!!

IT MUST HAVE BEEN A TOUGH DECISION...

NOT REALLY...

I CAN'T EVEN FIND THE DANG BLANG THINGS.

IRV, I NEED SOME BASIC TRANSPORTATION.

SURE. I THINK WE CAN FIX YOU RIGHT UP.

HOW 'BOUT THIS '59 CADDY?... A REAL CLEAN MACHINE...

NOPE. TOO FANCY... I'D LIKE TO SEE SOMETHING SENSIBLE...

WELL, THERE'S THIS PLYMOUTH CRANBROOK...

NOPE. I WANT A DEPENDABLE WAY TO GET AROUND — SOMETHING WITH GREAT GAS MILEAGE...

AHA...

BEHOLD THE NOBLE '48 CROSLEY!!

$350!

NO... I DON'T WANT TO SPEND THAT MUCH MONEY...

RIGHT.

I THINK I'VE GOT JUST THE THING.

A LITTLE OLD LADY USED THESE TO WALK TO BINGO EVERY WEDNESDAY.

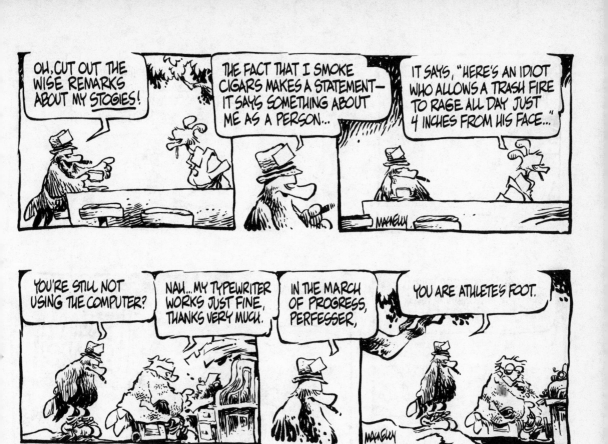

UH OH.... I THINK WE'RE IN TROUBLE...

COFFEE FUND

OUR COMPUTER REPAIRMAN HAS HIS OWN COFFEE CUP.

COFFEE FUND

ASK YOURSELVES, MY FRIENDS ... ARE YOU BETTER OFF TODAY THAN YOU WERE FOUR YEARS AGO?...

YOU ARE?

HOW DID THAT HAPPEN?

THIS REEGAN FELLA IS A REAL SLICKSTER, MY FRIENDS. SURE, HE'S A NICE GUY... AND HE COMES ACROSS REAL SMOOTH ON THE TUBE...

BUT DON'T BE FOOLED, FRIENDS...

BEHIND THAT AIR OF CONFIDENCE ...THE "AW, SHUCKS" SPEECHES, THE TINTED BRYLCREEM, THERE LURKS...

A REPUBLICAN.

Panel 1: PARDON ME, SIR... ARE YOU BETTER OFF TODAY THAN YOU WERE FOUR YEARS AGO?.

DARN RIGHT.

REALLY?

ABSOLUTELY.

Panel 2: 'COURSE, I WAS DOIN' TWO TO FIVE IN JOLIET AT THE TIME.

I PROMISE NOT TO RAISE TAXES...

I'VE ALWAYS BEEN AGAINST RAISING TAXES.

NOW TAXING RAISES— THAT'S ANOTHER THING.

WHAT'S UNCLE COSMO WORKING ON?

A PIECE OF FICTION.

I DIDN'T KNOW YOU PRINTED SHORT STORIES...

WE DON'T.

THAT'S HIS EXPENSE ACCOUNT.

THAT MUST BE THE SCULPTURE EXHIBIT I'M REVIEWING...

TREETOPS MUSEUM OF ART

SCULPTURE BY Sledge Zoomeister.

The new work by Master Sculptor Sledge Zoomeister is an interesting study in solidity—

A grouping of monolithic pieces which radiate a feeling of strength...

yet retain a mysterious airiness due to the simple, but deft use of positive and negative air space...

The solid concrete speaks of a solemn confidence — typical of Zoomeister's recent works...

but the friendly interaction of placement betrays the ominousness of the medium—displacing it with a light, familiarity of spirit — much like a squatting Stonehenge.

GOOD GRIEF!... I THINK I JUST REVIEWED THE NEW BENCHES.

MacNelly

History Test:
1. Who was Chester A. Arthur?

CHESTER A. WHO?

OH, WELL... HERE GOES...

Chester A. "Chet the Jet" Arthur was a left-handed relief pitcher for the Chicago White Sox from 1914 to 1919.

Famed for his remarkable side-arm "Doofus Pitch", Chet won 23 games in 1918 with 17 saves and 419 strikeouts...

Tragically, the talented southpaw was implicated in the infamous "Black Sox Scandal" in the 1919 World Series and mysteriously disappeared soon thereafter.

Arthur returned to baseball, however, during the 1926 season...

when he turned in Comiskey Park as a prize in a box of Crackerjacks.

LOOK. IF YOU HAVE TO GUESS, IT MIGHT AS WELL BE A WILD GUESS.

LISTEN, ROZ... I'M COUNTING MY CALORIES.

—ANY SUGGESTIONS?

TRY ONE OF THOSE STATE-OF-THE-ART CALCULATORS...

MACNELLY

History test: Who chopped down the cherry tree?

I CANNOT TELL A LIE.

Boy George did it.

MACNELLY

Math quiz:

What is 5 × 3.2 million?

The annual salary of the Lakers' starting lineup.

MACNELLY

Gentlemen:
When I subscribed to your fine magazine, I received a free quartz digital thermometer with leather case,

and the complimentary monogrammed tweezer set and Scratch-and-Sniff Atlas of the World.
But just one question:

When do I get the ☺*#? magazine?

MacNELLY

IS THERE ANYTHING ELSE ON THE TUBE, SKYLER?...

YEAH.

"Celebrity Blooper Thornbirds Fly the Winds of War to Rich Man, Poor Man's Texas Roots:

the continuing saga of a network in a desperate ratings race."

MacNELLY JR.

I'D LIKE TO SEE THE SCHOOL NURSE...

OKAY.

DO YOU HAVE BLUE CROSS-BLUE SHIELD?

NO. I THINK IT'S JUST PINKEYE...

THE OFFICE

THE OFFICE

MacNELLY

Dear Virginia:
    Yes, Virginia, there _is_ a Santa Claus.

It's a suburb of Los Angeles.

Thank you for writing the Tattler Tribune Action Line.

Dear Virginia:
    Thanks again for your letter. As I keep telling you, there _is_ a Santa Claus.

The reason he can fly all over the world for nothing is...

he's been in the Frequent Flyer Program for generations.

Dear Editor,
    Let me get this straight. You say there _is_ a Santa Claus, and he flies around the world in a sled at Christmas...

and gives _away_ millions of toys to boys and girls? How can he do it?
    — Virginia

Dear Virginia,
    Volume. Santa does enormous volume.

I KNOW EVERYONE IS LOOKING FORWARD TO SEEING US ON CHRISTMAS...

BUT I HATE FLYING ON HOLIDAYS...

WHAT DO YOU WANT MOST FOR CHRISTMAS, HUH, RUDY?

PUFF... PUFF...

I WANT BARREL BUTT BACK THERE TO TAKE UP JOGGING.

Police finally have a suspect in a bizarre series of nationwide laundry thefts.

They have not as yet obtained a confession in the case ...

but a search of the suspect's garage uncovered a pile of over three million unmatched socks.